This book is dedicated to my daughter Chloe,
and to my ginger tom-cat Alfie,
a never-ending source of annoyance
and inspiration.

First published in 1992 by
Kingfisher Books,
Grisewood & Dempsey Ltd,
Elsley House, 24-30 Great Titchfield Street,
London W1P 7AD

Copyright © 1992 by Gill Tomblin

Editor: Karen Filsell
Designer: Andrew Crowson

First published in the United States
by The Putnam & Grosset Book Group, New York.
Library of Congress Catalog Card Number: 91-61050
ISBN 0-399-22122-0
A B C D E F G H I J

Consultants:
Claire Robinson,
Education Officer, London Zoo
Michael Chinery

James G. Doherty
General Curator, The Bronx Zoo

Produced and directed by
David Bennett Books Ltd,
94 Victoria Street, St Albans,
Herts, AL1 3TG

Typesetting by Type City
Production by Imago
Printed in Singapore

Small and Furry Animals

A Watercolor Sketchbook of Mammals in the Wild

by Gill Tomblin

PUTNAM & GROSSET

Ever since I was a child, I've been curious about the everyday behavior of animals. Why, for instance, did my pleasure-loving cat, lazing in front of the fire, suddenly go out into the cold night to yowl and hiss at another cat on the garden wall? It was only much later, of course, I learned that cats mark their territory and this is the way they defend it against intruders.

As I grew up in England, country walks became adventures. I loved to see if I could tell which animals had been around—footprints in mud by a river might be those of a water vole, hair caught in a wire fence might be that of a fox or badger, and teeth marks in a mushroom might be the sign of a wood mouse's meal.

Actually seeing animals in the wild usually means waiting very patiently and quietly. I've sat and watched rabbits, quite unaware of my presence, nibbling the grass while one or two kept watch on their hind legs, sniffing the air. I've seen a badger at the same time every night, along one of his well-trodden routes, and I've caught fleeting glimpses of a fox returning to its den after its nightly hunt.

In Australia, where I lived for three years, I discovered possums would take nuts from my hand. They were almost as tame as gray squirrels in England which can be seen in every park, hurtling from tree to tree.

When I want to study more unusual or threatened animals, I go to wildlife sanctuaries or zoos. Here I can watch elegant lemurs being fed or see bushbabies bounding about as if they had springs on their feet. One of my favorite places is the night house, where nocturnal animals are kept in the quiet gloom. I can just see well enough to sketch how animals feed, move, and relate to one another.

I never get tired of watching and sketching animals. They are endlessly fascinating and I'm always discovering something new.

Gill Tomblin

CONTENTS

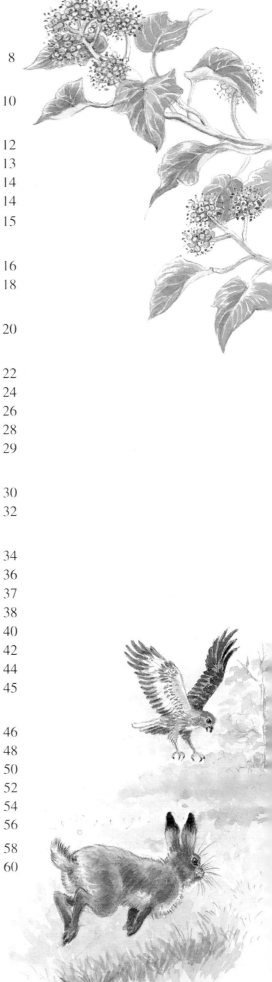

Introduction

The small, furry animals I have chosen for this book are all mammals, a group of animals which have certain features in common. Mammals have a backbone and skeleton inside their bodies, hair, and teeth. With the exception of the platypus and the spiny anteater, which both lay eggs, all mammals give birth to live young. The mothers nurse their young with their own milk, which is all the food the young need until they are ready to feed themselves. In fact, the word mammal comes from a Latin word, *mamma*, which means breast.

raccoon

Mammals are warm-blooded animals. This means they can keep their body temperature more or less the same whatever the weather. If they get too hot, they sweat or pant to cool down. In cool weather, their hair keeps them warm. Many mammals, particularly aquatic ones, have two kinds of hair. Close to their skin, they have soft, short underhair. Longer, coarser guard hairs on top trap a layer of air and stop their body heat from escaping.

sugar glider

snowshoe hare

Being warm-blooded enables mammals to live in almost every habitat on Earth—from the icy Arctic to hot deserts and steamy rain forests— wherever they can find a good supply of food. Mammals need to eat regularly so they have enough energy to keep themselves warm.

flying squirrel

Just by looking at a mammal, it is possible to tell quite a lot about where it lives and its habits. Mammals that live in trees, for example, usually have specially adapted limbs for climbing and gripping. Aquatic mammals, on the other hand, usually have streamlined bodies, powerful tails, and webbed feet. Many nocturnal animals have big eyes or ears to help them find food in the dark. Meat-eaters have sharp teeth for biting and tearing flesh, and plant-eaters have blunt teeth for grinding plants.

gray squirrel

douroucouli

There are more than four thousand different kinds of mammals. Scientists have divided them into groups which have similar features, such as pouches, wings, or grasping fingers. These groups are called orders and the different kinds of animals in each order are called species. For this book, I have chosen a few of my favorite species from the following orders:

Monotremes are mammals which lay soft-shelled eggs and have no teeth. There are only three living species of monotremes: the platypus, the long-beaked spiny anteater, and the short-beaked spiny anteater.

platypus

Marsupials give birth to tiny immature young which are hairless and blind. The newborn animals immediately attach themselves to a nipple on the mother's belly and stay there until they are fully formed. Some marsupials have a pouch for their young.

Virginia opossum

Insectivores are small, active, mainly nocturnal animals. They have small eyes and poor sight, but long, narrow sensitive snouts and a good sense of smell. They have numerous peg-like teeth and feed mainly on insects and other invertebrates.

common shrew

Bats are the only mammals capable of truly flying. The wings of bats are modified hands—the arm and finger bones are very elongated to support the wing membranes. There are almost a thousand species of bats.

pipistrelle

Primates are mostly tree-dwelling, sharp-sighted, intelligent mammals found mainly in tropical rain forests. They nearly all have flexible, grasping hands and feet. They also have bigger brains and live longer than most other mammals. Their young grow slowly and are dependent upon their parents for a relatively long time. Human beings are included in this order.

slow loris

Lagomorphs are ground-living animals with large ears and wide-set eyes. They are all herbivores and have two pairs of upper incisor teeth.

European brown hare

Rodents make up nearly forty percent of all mammal species and are found worldwide. They are mostly small and have frequent, large litters. Rodents have large, chisel-edged incisors, which grow continuously.

house mouse

Carnivores are mainly predatory meat-eating mammals. Their keen eyesight, hearing, and sense of smell help them find and catch prey. Carnivores generally have large, pointed canine teeth and sharp molars for holding and chewing meat.

European wild cat

9

PLATYPUS

broad, furry tail stores fat

burrow entrance

water-repellent fur

20in (50cm) head to tail

sensitive, rubbery bill for finding prey

The platypus is an unusual mammal. It lays eggs like reptiles and birds instead of giving birth to live young. But the young are warm-blooded and hairy, and the mother suckles them on milk like other mammals. The platypus lives in the rivers of eastern Australia and Tasmania. Its streamlined body is well adapted for swimming, since it finds its food underwater. It builds a burrow in a riverbank where it lives alone.

When courting, platypuses swim around in circles. The male tries to catch the female's tail in his bill.

The female builds a nest where she lays two soft, sticky eggs. After ten days, the eggs hatch.

Baby platypuses suck the milk that oozes through pores in their mother's belly. They learn to swim when they are four months old.

25ft (7.5m)

breeding burrow plugged with soil for safety

At dawn and dusk, the platypus comes out of its burrow to feed on prawns, crayfish, and insect larvae. It can stay underwater without breathing for up to ten minutes.

Because its eyes and ears are shut underwater, the platypus finds food by feeling in the mud with its bill. It brings its food up to the surface to eat.

hind feet used for steering

front feet used as paddles

tail used as rudder

The platypus grooms itself standing up. Its tail helps it to balance.

On land, the platypus walks on its knuckles.

webbed front paw used for swimming

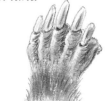

claws of front paw come out for digging on land

hind foot of male with poisoned spur for self-defense

The adult has no teeth. Instead, its bill has ridged pads for chewing.

MARSUPIALS
KOALA

thick fur on back for extra warmth in windy treetops

tufted ears

Koalas are found in Australia, where they live in the branches of eucalyptus trees. They sleep eighteen hours a day and feed mainly at night. They are very picky eaters, and choose only particular kinds of eucalyptus leaves. The female koala gives birth to one baby each year. A newborn koala is the size of a fingernail. It crawls into a pouch on its mother's belly and stays there for six months, drinking milk and growing. It lives with its mother until it is one year old.

big, sensitive nose for sniffing leaves

body length 2ft (60cm)

NEW SOUTH WALES KOALA

Koalas eat about two pounds of eucalyptus leaves each day. They rarely drink, because they get enough water from the leaves.

The baby koala hangs on tightly to its mother as she leaps from tree to tree.

hand *foot* *claws used as comb for grooming*

opposable big toe

Koalas can climb more than 148ft (45m) to the top of a tree.

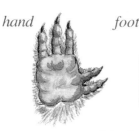

two opposable thumbs and claws for firm grip

POSSUM and GLIDER

large ears and eyes

long, sharp claws for gripping branches

body length 2ft (60cm)

Possums and gliders are Australian nocturnal tree dwellers, which have strong hands and feet. Possums also have prehensile tails which help them move easily through the trees.

BRUSH-TAILED POSSUM

The brush-tailed possum lives in woodlands, where it sleeps during the day in tree hollows. At night, it feeds on leaves, buds, insects, and small animals.

The baby brush-tailed possum clings to the nipple in its mother's pouch until it is five months old.

SUGAR GLIDER

A sugar glider gets its name because it feeds on the sweet blossoms of eucalyptus trees. When it leaps into the air, the skin between its front and hind legs stretches out like a parachute. Its tail is used for balance and steering.

HONEY POSSUM

The tiny honey possum reaches inside flowers with its long, bristly tongue and licks up nectar and pollen.

body length 3in (8cm)

13

WOMBAT

The wombat spends the day asleep in a burrow near the edge of a forest. At night it grazes or digs for roots. It can survive on a poor diet in times of drought.

HAIRY NOSED WOMBAT

long, silky fur

pouch opens backwards to prevent baby from being hit by flying soil

teeth grow all the time, but are constantly worn down by gnawing

body length up to 3½ ft (1m)

strong paws for digging

food is stored in cheek pouches

NUMBAT

The numbat hunts for termites, catching thousands of them each day. It lives and hunts alone.

The numbat does not have a pouch for its babies. Instead, they hang on nipples on their mother's belly.

striped and spotted coat provides camouflage in the woods

body length up to 11in (27cm)

sharp claws for ripping logs open

At the sound of danger, the numbat stands upright and gets ready to run.

pointed snout and long, sticky tongue for reaching termites

MARSUPIALS
OPOSSUM

VIRGINIA OPOSSUM

The Virginia opossum is the only marsupial in North America. It is slow-moving, like most nocturnal animals. Its toes and tail make it a good climber. The Virginia opossum nests in tree hollows, in rock crevices, or under fallen logs. It eats almost anything—birds, insects, fruit, worms, and even the contents of trash cans.

nest

hand with sharp claws for gripping bark

foot with opposable big toe

long, silky fur

body length up to 20in (50cm)

When faced with danger from a dog or a fox, the Virginia opossum "plays dead," sometimes for hours. Its predator usually loses interest.

Baby opossums cling to their mother's back for a month after leaving her pouch.

Up to twenty young are born at one time, but half of them die on the way to their mother's pouch. If the pouch is too crowded, a nipple may be pulled outside.

Opossums have prehensile tails.

SHREW

body length up to
3in (8cm)

long snout

Shrews are solitary animals. They search day and night for food. They use up so much energy that they must eat every two to three hours or they will die. Shrews have very poor eyesight, so they use their whiskers and good sense of smell to find food.

sensitive
whiskers

EUROPEAN WATER SHREW

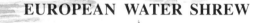

stiff hairs on feet trap water,
making feet like paddles

bristly tail acts as a rudder in water

A shrew builds a burrow in a riverbank, often with an underwater entrance.

As a wet shrew runs through the narrow tunnels of its burrow, its fur is brushed dry.

Freshwater snail shells and caddis fly cases are feeding signs of a water shrew.

A shrew has sharp teeth and poisonous saliva. Its bite paralyzes prey.

Underwater, the shrew is very buoyant because air is trapped under its fur. It paddles hard to catch its prey.

The common shrew finds food
among leaves and in tunnels that
it digs underground. It feeds on
worms, caterpillars, flies,
beetles, and woodlice.

*body length
2¹/₂ in (6cm)*

COMMON SHREW

The shrew uses its claws and teeth
for grooming. In spring, it sheds its
dark winter fur and grows a shorter,
light-colored summer coat.

The female builds a nest
inside a burrow. Each year
she has one or more litters
of four to seven young.

Before
they become
independent, young
shrews follow their mother by forming a chain.

Each common shrew has its own feeding
territory which it defends fiercely from
other hungry shrews. A shrew advances
on an intruder until their whiskers touch.
If the intruder does not retreat, both
shrews stand up and squeak.

After that, they roll onto their backs,
wriggling, squeaking, and grabbing
for each other's tail. They don't really
hurt each other.

Finally, one shrew
gives up and runs away.

17

INSECTIVORES
MOLE

sensitive tail

Moles are found in Europe, Asia and North America. They live almost entirely underground, and are especially well-suited for burrowing. They have powerful shoulders and forefeet, with strong, pointed claws for digging. Their fur is so short and smooth that they can move equally well forwards or backwards in their tunnels. They can even roll over to change direction.

very poor eyesight

velvety fur

body length 5in (13cm)

EUROPEAN MOLE

long snout and whiskers help find earthworms by touch

forearm has extra finger-like bone for digging

The female enlarges one of her tunnels to build a breeding nest, which she lines with leaves and grass. Three or four young are born there in the spring.

large fortress molehill covering breeding nest

molehills

nest has several exits

Moles hunt and feed for four hours, rest for another four hours, and then go hunting again.

store of live worms, heads bitten off by mole

After burrowing a distance, a European mole digs a vertical tunnel to the surface. It pushes the loose excavated soil out of the tunnel to form a molehill.

Mole tunnels are very narrow. As the mole rushes through them, its fur becomes clean and sleek.

The European mole lives by itself. It patrols its tunnels several times each day in search of food and fiercely chases away any intruders.

In wet weather, underground burrows may flood. The mole paddles to land using its long nose like a snorkel.

NORTH AMERICAN STAR-NOSED MOLE

The American star-nosed mole swims well and catches most of its food in the water. It feeds on shrimps, small fish, insect larvae, and earthworms.

long tail

The mole has a ring of twenty-two tentacles around its snout, which it waves around in search of food.

body length up to 8in (20cm)

underwater entrance to burrow

BAT

free thumb with claw

Bats are found in all parts of the world except cold polar regions, and there are over 950 species of them. They are all nocturnal and are the only mammals that can fly. Fruit bats live in tropical countries and use their large eyes to find their way about. Insect-eating bats live in temperate and tropical countries. They have large ears and catch insects using echolocation. There are also bats which catch fish, hunt rodents, or drink the blood of large mammals.

GRAY-HEADED FRUIT BAT

The fruit bat pierces the skin of ripe bananas, dates, guavas, and figs with its sharp teeth. Then it sucks out the flesh.

PIPISTRELLE

Pipistrelle bats usually have one young at a time. The young bat clings to its mother as she flies, until it becomes too heavy for her.

body length 2in (5cm)

wingspan 9in (23cm)

Many mothers and babies hang together in nursery roosts inside buildings or caves, or on trees.

By hooking its thumbs into tree bark and pushing with its feet, the bat can crawl along a branch or even up a vertical tree trunk.

The pipistrelle bat has poor eyesight. It finds its way in the dark with the help of its large ears. As it flies, it makes very high-pitched clicking noises, too high for humans to hear. It listens for echoes that bounce off any prey or obstacle in its path. The echoes tell the bat where to fly and where to find food. This is called echolocation.

The pipistrelle flies with fast, fluttery movements in search of flying insects, usually gnats or moths.

The pipistrelle catches one insect at a time. It scoops it up with its tail, and bends over to eat it.

In winter, when insects are scarce, pipistrelle bats hibernate in cool places. Their body temperature drops until beads of condensation form on their fur.

GREATER HORSESHOE BAT

This bat squeaks through its nostrils, which act like a megaphone.

LONG-EARED BAT

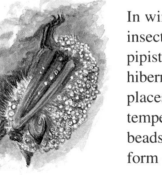

The long ears of this bat help it echolocate especially well.

SANBORN'S LONG-NOSED BAT

This bat has a long snout and rough tongue. It hovers over flowers to feed on their nectar and pollen.

21

LEMUR

Lemurs live only in the forests of Madagascar, an island near East Africa. There are over twenty kinds. The ring-tailed lemur is one of the most common. It is about the size of a domestic cat. Ring-tails live in family groups headed by females. They forage for fruit and leaves to eat and sleep in the trees at night.

RING-TAILED LEMUR

On the ground, a ring-tail keeps its tail in the air, like a flag. This lets the rest of the group know where it is.

tamarind fruit, a favorite food of all lemurs

A young ring-tail uses its tail to hold tight to its mother, while she uses hers as a blanket.

A ring-tail's arms and legs are nearly the same length. It can run along the ground on all fours.

The mother carries her baby on her back wherever she goes for about six months.

22

During the mating season, two ring-tails may have a stink fight for a female. Each male rubs his wrists against smelly glands in his armpits and then along his tail. The two rivals then fan each other with their smelly tails.

One male may give in, or a fierce fight may follow to see who will win the female.

sharp claw used as earpick

foot

short nails for picking fruit

hand

Ring-tails have strong, nimble hands and feet, both with opposable thumbs.

Ring-tails often sit upright on the ground to sunbathe. They usually sit in groups.

23

NEW WORLD MONKEYS

New World monkeys live high in the trees of South American rain forests. Because they are small, light, and very agile, they are ideally suited for climbing and leaping. They have good eyesight and can spot the flowers, fruit, and nuts they eat from far away. They are mainly active during the day, when they can see where they are going.

SQUIRREL MONKEY

hands and feet with long, pointed nails for gripping bark

body length 10in (25cm)

tail length 16in (40cm)

tail used for balance when leaping

Squirrel monkeys travel in family groups. They hurl themselves from tree to tree, sometimes leaping as far as 25ft (7.5m). They also leap into the air to catch flying insects.

The underside of a prehensile tail has no hair. It has a ridged surface that can grip branches just like a hand.

SPIDER MONKEY

The spider monkey can hang by its tail.

The female has one baby at a time, who rides on her back until it is independent.

curved hands and long, thin toes for grasping branches

body length up to 2ft (60cm)

The hand of a spider monkey is unusual because it has no thumb.

foot

hand

CAPUCHIN MONKEY

DOUROUCOULI

The douroucouli is the only nocturnal monkey. It can see three times as well as humans in the dark.

Like all monkeys, capuchin monkeys spend a lot of time carefully grooming their young to keep them clean.

25

TAMARIN and MARMOSET

Tamarins and marmosets are very small, rare monkeys who live in the rain forests of South America. They are slim, agile climbers with sharp claws on their hands and feet. During the day they can be very vocal, producing high-pitched calls. They eat insects, fruit, and flowers.

GOLDEN LION TAMARIN

*body length
8in (20cm)*

bright golden fur

*slender fingers
with sharp claws
for gripping bark*

*long tail
for balance*

Newborn tamarins cling to their father's fur.

Tamarins live in family groups with a mother, father, and their offspring. The father takes care of the young most of the time. He hands them over to the mother when it is time for feeding.

COMMON MARMOSET

Marmosets are great leapers.

A young marmoset rides on its father's back. At two months, it can travel on its own.

During the day, marmosets rest along branches. At night, they sleep in holes in tree trunks.

Marmosets and tamarins hang upside down by digging their claws into branches.

Males are aggressive when defending their territory. They arch their backs and bare their teeth to keep other males away.

hand with long fingers and sharp claws

Marmosets use their claws and teeth to groom each other.

foot with claws and short big toe with flat nail

BUSHBABY

Bushbabies live in Africa. They are so named because they make a cry like a human baby. They rest all day in groups, curled up on a branch or in a nest of leaves. At night, they split up and hunt alone for insects, lizards, and birds' eggs. They also eat fruit and sip tree sap.

large ears

large eyes

hand

flattened fingers for climbing and grasping

body length 16in (40cm) including tail

SENEGAL BUSHBABY

A bushbaby is a fast and agile leaper. It has strong hind legs and can leap up to 20ft (6m) between trees. Its long tail helps it to balance and brake. It lands upright, gripping the tree trunk.

strong, furry tail used as a rudder

Bushbabies use their incredibly sharp hearing to find insects in the dark.

The mother stays close to her newborn baby for a few weeks, but she leaves it in the nest when she hunts.

LORIS

thick, woolly fur   *large eyes*

Lorises are nocturnal animals that live in the tropical forests of Asia. They stay high up in the trees, rarely coming down to the ground. They creep slowly along branches in search of insects, trying not to shake twigs or leaves which might give them away. Lorises have very short tails that are hidden under their thick fur. Since they move so slowly, they have no need of a tail for balance.

body length 15in (38cm)

SLOW LORIS

strong, muscular legs and feet

The mother parks her baby on a branch while she hunts.

Lorises eat many bad-tasting caterpillars and other insects that most animals won't touch. They creep toward their prey until it is within reach and then suddenly lunge forward to grasp it.

hand with opposable thumb

Lorises drink dew by dipping their fingers in wet leaves and then licking them.

Lorises have a network of blood vessels in their limbs which slow down the blood flow. This means they can remain still for hours at a time.

LAGOMORPHS
RABBIT

Rabbits are found in many parts of the world. They eat mainly grasses, but also twigs and bark. Some rabbits live alone or in small groups, making their homes in shallow holes, called forms, on the ground. Others live in large groups in underground tunnels called warrens.

EUROPEAN RABBIT

soft, dense fur

long, mobile ears for sharp hearing

European rabbits come out to feed at dawn and dusk, rarely moving far from the warren.

large eyes set far apart for wide field of vision

body length 16in (40cm)

short tail with white underside

Young rabbits, called kittens, are born naked and blind. They emerge from their nest at three weeks, fully furred.

breeding nest lined with fur from female

sleeping burrow

rabbit warren

A rabbit stands on its hind legs to get a better view. It turns its head from side to side to catch the scent, sight, or sound of predators.

At the first sign of a predator, rabbits dash for their burrow. They flash the white underside of their tails to warn other rabbits of the danger.

30

A rabbit moves in a series of short hops with one forepaw slightly in front of the other. Its powerful hind legs are much longer than the forelegs.

tracks of forefeet   *tracks of hind feet*

Rabbits digest their food twice to get all the nutrients from it. While underground in the daytime, a rabbit swallows the first set of droppings it passes. It then leaves a second set of droppings outside the burrow entrance.

A male rabbit marks his territory by rubbing the ground with the scent gland on his chin.

European rabbits often damage trees by eating the bark. They eat the bark all the way around, causing young trees to die.

MARSH COTTONTAIL

EASTERN COTTONTAIL

The Eastern cottontail is found in much of Central and North America. It rests in a form in the grass. When in danger, the cottontail sometimes finds safety in the unused burrow of another animal.

The marsh cottontail rabbit makes a nest in marshy areas. If threatened, it lies motionless on its back in the water. Only its eyes, nose, and mouth remain above the surface.

walking tracks of a marsh cottontail

31

LAGOMORPHS
HARE

long ears

form

powerful hind legs

Brown hares are solitary, cautious animals. They live unsheltered in open pastures. Their only protection is their form, which they make in the grassy undergrowth. Brown hares have thick fur which keeps them warm. Sharp hearing and eyesight keep them alert to danger, and they can run very fast to escape.

EUROPEAN BROWN HARE

body length 2ft (60cm)

A brown hare lies motionless, hiding from danger.

Brown hares usually have two young in a litter, but may have three litters in a year. The young, called leverets, are born fully furred and with their eyes open.

Males, called jacks, compete for females in the spring. They turn in circles and box each other with their paws until one of them gives up.

32

If a brown hare sights a hawk, it runs away as fast as it can. It can run as fast as 35mph (56km/h).

When the hawk swoops down, the hare suddenly jumps out of the way and the bird crash-lands. Hares can jump as high as 6½ft (2m).

Brown hares feed mainly at dusk and dawn on grass and vegetables. They eat their first set of soft droppings to give them extra nutrients.

large incisors with space behind them for carrying food and bedding

SNOWSHOE HARE

In spring, the snowshoe hare loses its white coat and grows a reddish-brown coat for the summer.

The snowshoe hare lives in Canada and the northern United States. In winter, it feeds on twigs and bark, and roots that it finds beneath the snow.

The soles of its hind feet are covered with thick hair to help grip snow. These "snowshoes" also keep the hare's feet warm.

BEAVER

*body length
up to 3½ ft (1m)*

*sharp teeth for
gnawing wood*

*long guard hairs
keep water out
and heat in*

*flat, scaly tail
for steering*

Beavers live by riverbanks in the forests of North America and parts of Europe. They are aquatic rodents who are well-known for their building skills. With their sharp teeth they gnaw down trees and cut up logs to build dams and homes called lodges. Beavers live in family groups made up of parents and offspring. The young, known as kits, leave to make their own homes after about two years.

NORTH AMERICAN BEAVER

Beavers build their lodges near alder, poplar, willow, and aspen trees, which grow by riverbanks. They use bigger, older branches for building and eat the shoots of young branches.

lodge

*winter stockpile of twigs
pushed firmly into mud*

*underwater
entrance*

*dam made of logs,
twigs, and mud*

Beavers dig canals from their lodges so they can fetch wood from further afield when their local supply runs out.

The beaver slaps its tail against the water to warn other beavers when predators threaten the lodge.

tail raised to change direction

webbed hind feet for speed underwater

A beaver can stay below the surface for fifteen minutes before coming up to breathe. Its eyes are protected by a transparent skin so it can see underwater.

forefeet tucked under chin while swimming

A beaver gnaws all around a tree trunk and then runs out of the way when the tree falls. It may be crushed if it is not quick enough. The branches are gnawed into small lengths for building and eating.

hind foot

forefoot

cone-shaped stumps left by beaver

large incisors protected by extra-hard, rust-colored enamel

A beaver can close its lips behind its incisors so it can gnaw and carry sticks underwater without choking.

A beaver stands upright to carry a tired kit.

Young kits cannot dive. Instead, they are carried underwater on their mother's back.

TREE SQUIRREL

drey

Gray squirrels spend much of their time scurrying about in the treetops, feeding on nuts, shoots, and fruit. At night, and in cold and rainy weather, they rest in a nest, called a drey, made of leaves, twigs, and bark. Gray squirrels are native to the eastern United States. They were introduced to England a hundred years ago and are now a familiar sight there in parks and gardens.

GRAY SQUIRREL

The female gray squirrel lines the drey with soft leaves and moss. Her young are born there naked, blind, and deaf.

*body length
up to 20in (50cm)
including tail*

*wide-angle
vision*

*powerful
hind legs and long
hind feet for climbing*

*keen
sense of
smell*

*sharp claws
for gripping bark*

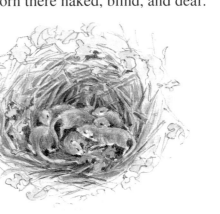

tail used as rudder

The gray squirrel bounds from branch to branch quickly and easily. When it leaps to the ground, it lands on its forefeet and its tail flips overhead.

*hazelnut
opened
by young gray
squirrel*

Gray squirrels strip the bark from trees and feed on the sappy wood underneath.

*hazelnut
opened
cleanly by adult
gray squirrel*

Gray squirrels hide nuts and seeds for the winter. They may also raid bird feeders in the cold weather when food is scarce.

FLYING SQUIRREL

*body length 14in
(37cm) including tail*

Flying squirrels are the only nocturnal squirrels. There are over three dozen species of them found in the forests of North America, Europe, Japan, and Southeast Asia. Their front and hind legs are connected by a furry fold of skin on either side of the body. When the squirrel leaps, it stretches out its limbs and the skin acts like a parachute, enabling the squirrel to glide 100 feet (30m) or more through the air.

NORTHERN FLYING SQUIRREL

*feathery tail for
balance and steering*

A young squirrel often falls when learning to glide. The mother rescues it, picking it up by its fold of skin.

Flying squirrels rest in tree hollows during the day. In winter, several rest together to keep warm.

cocked head

*limbs outstretched
in flight*

*tail raised and body upright,
ready to land*

*landing on all fours,
clawed toes
grasping
bark*

Before the squirrel takes off, it cocks its head from side to side to judge the distance to its landing spot. Then it pushes away from the tree with its back legs, leaps into the air, and spreads its limbs out wide.

In autumn, flying squirrels store nuts by wedging them into tree crevices.

*darting around
to far side of tree
in case a predator
is watching*

37

PRAIRIE DOG

The prairie dog's name comes from its call, which sounds like the bark of a dog. But prairie dogs are actually ground-living squirrels. They live on the grassy plains of North America in huge "towns" with as many as one thousand prairie dogs. Each town is divided into family units called coteries, made up of one male, several females, and their pups. A coterie has its own system of burrows which is passed from one generation to the next.

blunt nose

small ears for ease in tunnelling

short tail for balance

body length up to 16in (40cm)

burrow entrance

BLACK-TAILED PRAIRIE DOG

Mounds of earth at burrow entrances serve as lookout posts and help to prevent flooding.

coterie members on watch at burrow entrances

guard sounding alarm at approach of hawk

listening post

chamber used during floods

sleeping chamber

latrine

prairie dog carrying bedding

Prairie dogs maintain the mounds around their burrows. Nose prints can be seen where they have pressed down the soil.

During the breeding season, females set up their own nesting territories. Young males are forced out by the females and have to dig new burrows on the outskirts of the colony.

Sometimes a badger and a coyote work together to capture a prairie dog. One animal flushes it from the burrow. The other waits quietly nearby to catch it.

tail flips up while calling

Prairie dog pups roam outside their territory and kiss and nuzzle every prairie dog they meet. As they get older, they are rejected by dogs from other coteries. This way, they learn the boundaries of their own territory.

A prairie dog has different calls for different predators. Once danger is past, it jumps up to give an all-clear call.

39

DESERT RODENTS

Rodents are the most common desert mammals. They are largely nocturnal, and rest in burrows during the day to avoid the extreme heat. They do not need to drink very much because their bodies can conserve the moisture they get from their food.

DESERT JERBOA

large earbones amplify sound

body length 10in (25cm) including tail

sand-colored fur provides camouflage

long tail for better balance on two feet

short forefeet with claws

very long hind legs

hair on underside of foot prevents sinking in sand

large feet

emergency exit

main entrance

The desert jerboa lives in African and Asian deserts. Each jerboa digs its own burrow. The main entrance is blocked with sand to keep out the hot, dry air and to conserve moisture.

MONGOLIAN GERBIL

This species of gerbil has become a popular pet.

Males stand on their hind legs to fight over territory.

Mongolian gerbils are sociable and share a burrow. The moisture from their breath collects in their chamber and prevents it from drying out.

KANGAROO RAT

Kangaroo rats live in the deserts of North America, where they often fall prey to owls and snakes. Their hearing is four times sharper than human hearing. At the faintest sound, they jump for safety. They can jump as far as 20ft (6m) in one second.

If a kangaroo rat hears a predator, it takes off, its tail streaming downward.

It can change direction in midair, using its tail as a rudder.

As the rat lands, it raises its tail, which acts like a brake.

To keep its fur clean and free from parasites, the kangaroo rat takes regular sand baths.

The kangaroo rat has fur-lined cheek pouches. On foraging trips, it picks up seeds with its front paws and fills its pouches.

During the day, the kangaroo rat rests in a burrow mound. The entrances are plugged for safety and to keep the air inside moist and cool.

forefeet

hind feet

tail drag

track of hopping kangaroo rat

lower bones of a rat's hind feet, fused together for strength and support when jumping

Back at its burrow, the kangaroo rat hits its cheeks to release the food.

41

MOUSE

large, erect ears

large eyes

There are many species of mice found all over the world. All of them are active and inquisitive. They breed frequently and can have several litters in a year. Mice mainly eat seeds, roots, grasses, and berries, but some also eat insects or worms.

WOOD MOUSE

body length 7in (18cm) including tail

wide feet

a wood mouse's burrow

food store

long tail for balance

During the day, the wood mouse rests in an underground burrow.

breeding nest

At night, it carries leaves to the nest to use for bedding.

Babies are born mainly in spring and summer, with as many as five or six in a litter.

jumping tracks in the snow

hind feet

forefeet

NORTH AMERICAN WHITE-FOOTED MOUSE

North American white-footed mice make their homes in any hidden place, such as an old bird's nest.

tail drag

plum pit neatly opened by wood mouse

HOUSE MOUSE

nest of newspaper

The female may have up to ten litters of three to five young each year.

body length 4in (10cm)

House mice are found wherever humans live, and where there is plenty of food and shelter.

If house mice are overcrowded, they become very aggressive, and males will fight for dominance.

EUROPEAN HARVEST MOUSE

The tiny, nimble harvest mouse lives among the tall grasses of fields and meadows. In early summer, it builds a nest above ground, safe from predators. It eats flowers, fruit, seeds, and grains.

body length 5in (13cm) including tail

To build its nest, the mouse shreds the ends of grass blades which are still attached to their stems.

Then it weaves the blades into a tight ball, firmly attached to the stems of grass on either side.

The harvest mouse grips a stalk with its hind feet and prehensile tail. This leaves its forefeet free for feeding.

43

RAT

There are several hundred species of rats living in every part of the world except the polar regions. They breed rapidly—a single brown rat can have up to fifty young a year, and her young can breed when they are only three months old.

WOODRAT

large eyes and ears

furry tail

forefoot

long whiskers

hind foot

body length 18in (46cm) including tail

The woodrat, also known as the packrat, is found in North America and Mexico. It builds its nest out of all kinds of objects, such as tin cans, bones, and even spoons.

BROWN RAT

Brown rats are often found in urban areas, and are probably the most adaptable animals ever. They are excellent swimmers and many live in city sewers. In the country, they sometimes build burrows in riverbanks.

Brown rats live wherever they can find plenty of food, water and shelter. They will eat almost anything, but they test small amounts of unfamiliar food to make sure it is safe to eat.

A family of brown rats share a scent that they transfer to one another. First one rat sniffs another, then it creeps under the other's raised leg.

RODENTS
VOLE

small ears hidden in fur

Voles are small, scurrying animals that are active day and night, alternating between feeding and resting. They have many predators and rarely survive longer than a year or two.

EUROPEAN BANK VOLE

The tiny bank vole lives in woodlands and hedges, where it finds shelter in the thick undergrowth.

squat, rounded body

body length 4in (10cm)

short legs

nest *food store*

nuts hollowed out by bank vole

The bank vole climbs bushes and brambles to feed on fruit, seeds, leaves, and flowers. It also eats insects.

The young are born blind and naked. They spend their first few weeks in an underground nest lined with grass, moss, and wool.

EUROPEAN WATER VOLE

The water vole lives on riverbanks and feeds on grasses and other plants. It digs a burrow in the bank where it sleeps and stores food.

footprints

body length 8in (20cm)

chewed grasses

Fox

pointed ears

RED FOX

*eyes adapted
for night vision*

Red foxes are resourceful animals, common in North America, Europe, Asia, and Australia. Although they are wild animals, they sometimes live near people. Adult red foxes live in pairs, or in groups with one male, called a dog fox, and several females, called vixens.

body length 3½ ft (1m)

den

*bushy tail with
scent gland*

The vixen gives birth in a den built underground. The dog fox brings food to her.

Some vixens have no young, but help look after the cubs of other vixens.

Older cubs follow their parents on foraging trips. They learn how to locate earthworms by poking their noses into the grass.

If she senses danger, the vixen carries young cubs by the scruff of the neck to a safe den.

Red foxes may come into suburban yards and scavenge in garbage cans for scraps to eat.

Red foxes follow the same paths every night in search of food. They leave fresh droppings as scent markers.

Dog foxes sometimes fight for dominance. They stand on their hind legs and push one another, barking loudly. The fights rarely end in bloodshed.

When a red fox hears the rustling of a mouse or vole, it leaps into the air and pins the prey down with both forepaws.

Extra food is often buried in a hole that a red fox digs with its forepaws. The fox may return to the hole when food is scarce.

MEERKAT

Meerkats inhabit the dry sandy plains of southern Africa. They live in colonies and dig burrows with lots of entrances and deep passageways. Meerkats come out of their burrows at daybreak to feed, but never wander far from home. When the local food supply runs out, the whole colony moves to new feeding grounds and digs new burrows.

good eyesight and sense of smell

slender body covered with long, soft fur

ears that close to keep out sand

striped fur on back

body length 21in (55cm) including tail

tapered tail

short legs

SLENDER-TAILED MEERKAT

Meerkats stand on their hind legs to look over tall grasses for possible predators.

A litter of three or four young is born in a grass-lined nest in the burrow. Newborn meerkats are blind and have no fur. After a month, the babies come out of the burrow.

The whole family looks after the young meerkats. Older brothers and sisters play with them. The mother and father groom and protect the young and take them on foraging trips to teach them which foods to eat.

Meerkats go foraging in small groups. They scrape the earth in search of centipedes, insects, spiders, lizards, and roots. They make purring sounds to keep in touch with each other.

When a meerkat spots dangerous prey, it moves forward with its back arched and its tail in the air. It can be very aggressive and can kill a small mammal or snake with its bite.

If a meerkat catches a scorpion, it bites off its stinging tail before killing and eating it.

Meerkats spend much of the day basking in the sun. When they get too hot, they lie face down in a cool burrow.

A few meerkats keep watch for predators, such as hawks and eagles. They stand as high up as possible so they have a good view. At the first sight of danger, the guards let out a shrill bark, and all the meerkats dash for their burrows.

BADGER

Eurasian badgers are squat, powerful animals with strong claws for digging. They live in family groups and build deep burrow systems, called setts, in woody areas. At dusk, they come out to feed. Earthworms are their main diet, but they also eat fruit, roots, plants, and small animals.

well-trodden paths to feeding grounds

sharpening claws

EURASIAN BADGER

cubs playing by sett entrance

body length 3ft (90cm) including tail

coarse gray hair

black and white head markings for visibility in the dark

dung-pits marking edge of territory

blunt snout and good sense of smell

short forelegs and long, sturdy claws for digging

old bedding

A litter of one to four Eurasian badger cubs is born between January and March. The cubs stay underground for eight weeks.

stored bedding

sleeping chamber

breeding chamber

Eurasian badgers are wary of people, but they will sometimes go into gardens at night if food is provided for them. They especially like bread, honey, peanuts, and raisins.

Eurasian badgers raise their tails to spread scent on each other. The scent helps them identify those in their group.

Males may attack strangers venturing onto their territory. An angry badger bares its teeth and fluffs up its fur, which makes it look bigger.

AMERICAN BADGER

American badgers have flatter bodies than Eurasian badgers, and their head markings are different. They live alone in shallow burrows and hunt rodents and rabbits.

An American badger defends itself by blocking the entrance to its burrow with its wide body. It uses its claws to fight off attackers.

body length 3ft (90cm) including tail

51

OTTER

small ears

*body length
4ft (1.2m)
including tail*

short legs

*otter in lookout position,
balanced on feet and tail*

Otters are playful
aquatic mammals. Their
large lungs and streamlined
bodies enable them to swim fast
underwater in search of prey.

COMMON OTTER

*chamber above
flood level*

A common otter lives by freshwater
rivers and lakes across Europe and
parts of Asia and Japan. Its home
is called a holt. The entrance is in
a riverbank, hidden by tree roots.

underwater entrance

*strong,
tapered tail*

*webbed
feet*

When the otter comes out of the water,
it shakes itself and rolls around.
Then it grooms itself to keep
its coat glossy.

Common otters can stay underwater
for four minutes. They can see
as well underwater as on land.

Common otters are playful both on land and in the water. They make slides on wet or snowy riverbanks.

Common otter cubs don't go into the water until they are four months old and their coats are waterproof. Their mother has to push them into the water for their first swim.

An otter likes to toss a pebble and catch it in its mouth.

A common otter holds its prey while it eats. Its main food is fish.

SEA OTTER

The sea otter lives in shallow waters off the coasts of California and Alaska. It comes ashore only during storms.

body length 6ft (1.8m) including tail

After diving for shellfish, sea urchins, and crabs, the sea otter floats on its back to eat.

At night, the sea otter wraps kelp around its body to keep from drifting away in fast-moving currents.

53

RACCOON

distinctive mask-like coloring around eyes

hand-like forepaws

clawed toes

striped tail

long, thick fur

body length 3ft (90cm) including tail

At one time, raccoons lived mainly in North American forests, making their dens in tree hollows and rock crevices. Recently, however, they have adapted to life in the open country, and even in towns. In towns, they may roam in groups and scavenge to survive. In the wild, raccoons are solitary and jealously guard their food supplies.

A litter of three or four cubs is born in the spring, fully furred. At first, they are blind and helpless. Their mother suckles them for two months, until they are ready to go foraging.

In times of danger, the mother carries her cubs by the scruff of their necks to a safer place.

54

Raccoons are very curious and use
their nimble forepaws to open doors,
turn knobs, and lift trash can lids.

Raccoons sometimes hunt at night
in shallow water for shellfish, mollusks,
frogs, and fish. They dabble underwater
with their sensitive fingers until they find prey.
Then they quickly scoop it out. They also eat
earthworms, insects, birds' eggs, and chicks,
as well as fruit, nuts, and berries.

forepaw

hind paw

In cold climates, raccoons grow
a thick coat and gain weight for the winter.
They sleep through the coldest days in their
den. In the southern United States, however,
raccoons stay active all year.

footprints

CAT

Wild cats survive mainly in remote parts of the world. They are silent, skillful hunters who walk on the pads of their toes to creep up quietly on their prey. Sharp claws and teeth also aid them in hunting.

JUNGLE CAT

pointed ears

forward-facing eyes for judging distances

long, sensitive whiskers

muscular legs and shoulders

claws in when stalking

The jungle cat lives in the forests and grasslands of Asia and the Middle East. It feeds on rodents and birds. The ancient Egyptians trained these cats to hunt for game.

A jungle cat tries to get as close as possible to its prey before it attacks. It flattens itself in the grass and prepares to leap.

It pounces on its prey and catches it with its claws.

EUROPEAN WILD CAT

The European wild cat is an extremely fierce member of the cat family. It is the ancestor of the domestic cat, but it is larger and has much thicker fur. European wild cats live alone in forests and on mountainsides, and hunt at night.

body length 2¹/₂ ft (77cm) including tail

hind paw with soft pads

forepaw with claws out

forepaw with pads, claws in

Like domestic cats, wild cats often scratch trees to exercise their muscles and sharpen their worn claws.

A female may mate with the same male twice a year. Her kittens are born in a grass-lined den which she makes in a hollow tree or rock crevice.

Kittens chase each other playfully and have mock fights.

SERVAL

The serval lives on the African savanna. It can run fast and leap high through long grass. It can even catch birds in midair.

body length 3¹/₂ ft (1m)

long, sensitive ears aid hunting at night

short, smooth hair

spotted coat provides camouflage

long legs

HABITATS

Savanna grasslands are found in the tropics where rain falls only in the summer and the temperature is high all year round. The tall grasses are ideal feeding grounds for enormous herds of grazing animals.

Savanna animals: Senegal bushbaby, serval

Cultivated grasslands have been colonized by a few small grazing animals. Since farming restricts plants to a few species, the number of different animals is also limited.

Cultivated grassland animals: European mole, European rabbit, eastern cottontail, European brown hare, house mouse, European harvest mouse

Australian grasslands have bushes and trees which provide food and shelter for different sorts of animals. The trees are mainly eucalyptus.

Australian grassland animals: honey possum, hairy-nosed wombat, koala

Prairies are regions covered with tall, thick grasses. Because there are few trees to provide cover, prairie animals must be constantly on guard for predators. Many animals live in large groups which helps protect them.

Prairie animals: prairie dog, American badger

Temperate woodlands have a mixture of trees, such as oak, beech, ash, and hickory, with shrubs and other plants growing beneath them. In autumn, most of the trees shed their leaves. The forest floor is covered with rotting leaves that teem with worms and insects, providing food for many small animals.

Temperate forest animals: brush-tailed possum, Virginia opossum, common shrew, European mole, pipistrelle, greater horseshoe bat, long-eared bat, gray squirrel, flying squirrel, wood mouse, European bank vole, red fox, Eurasian badger, raccoon, jungle cat, European wild cat

Evergreen forests have pine, spruce, and fir trees which grow thickly and block the sunlight so that few plants grow on the forest floor. Animals living here have thick coats to protect them during extremely cold winters.

Evergreen forest animals: snowshoe hare

Tropical rain forests are found near the Equator where the weather is constantly hot and rainy. In these hot, humid conditions, plants grow quickly and provide plenty of food and shelter for the widest variety of animals and insects in the world.

Tropical rain forest animals: gray-headed fruit bat, squirrel monkey, spider monkey, douroucouli, capuchin monkey, golden lion tamarin, common marmoset, slow loris, ring-tailed lemur

Deserts are regions where little rain falls and the soil is very dry. Few plants, therefore, can grow there. Desert animals have found ways to survive without much water.

Desert animals: numbat, desert jerboa, Mongolian gerbil, kangaroo rat, woodrat

Rivers and streams are homes for many small animals whose bodies are streamlined for swimming. Many of them build burrows in the riverbanks and find food in the water.

River animals: platypus, European water shrew, North American star-nosed mole, marsh cottontail, beaver, European water vole, common otter

Suburban gardens provide refuge for several small animals which may scavenge in trash cans for food.

Suburban garden animals: red fox, Eurasian badger, raccoon

59

GLOSSARY

Adapt The way an animal copes efficiently with its environment and so improves its chances of survival.

Aggressive Ready to fight.

red foxes fighting

Aquatic Growing, living, or found in water.

Breed To produce young.

Camouflage The way in which an animal's body covering helps it blend into surroundings so it can hide from enemies or creep up on its prey unnoticed.

Canine teeth The long pointed teeth on either side of the incisor teeth, used for holding, killing, and tearing. These are especially prominent in carnivores.

Carnivore A mammal that eats the flesh of other animals.

Colony A large group of the same species of animals which live together.

Dependent Relying on another animal, usually parents, for food and support.

Dominant The dominant animal in a group has the position of power and importance.

Forage Search for food.

Groom To clean by picking deep down in the hair.

capuchin monkeys grooming

Habitat The surroundings in which an animal lives, such as grassland or desert.

Herbivore A mammal that eats plants.

European rabbit feeding on grass

Hibernate A time of inactivity, rather like a deep sleep, during the cold winter months when there is little or no food available. When an animal hibernates, its heart rate and breathing slow down and its body temperature drops. It uses very little energy and survives on the fat it has built up in its body before hibernation.

Incisor teeth The long, flat, sharp teeth at the front of the mouth, particularly prominent in rodents.

skull of a beaver

incisor teeth

Independent Capable of living on its own.

Litter The offspring of a single mother, all born at the same time.

European wild cat nursing litter

Nocturnal A nocturnal animal is active at night and rests during the day.

Opposable Thumbs or toes which can move and turn freely, and touch the tips of the other fingers are called opposable. This is a feature of primates.

opposable thumb of a slow loris

Parasite An organism living in or on another.

Predator An animal that hunts and kills other animals for food.

Prehensile tail A muscular tail adapted for grasping like a hand. It is usually bald on the gripping side.

Prey An animal which is hunted and eaten by other animals.

Scent gland A part of the body which produces smelly substances used to attract others of the opposite sex. Also used to mark territory.

Skull The bony skeleton protecting the head of a mammal.

skull of a hare

Social Living in a group.

Solitary Living alone.

Species A kind of animal. Animals in a species can breed together.

Streamlined Shaped to move easily through the water or the air.

Territory An area of land which animals mark out as their own and defend against other animals.

Warren A network of underground tunnels and chambers in which rabbits live.

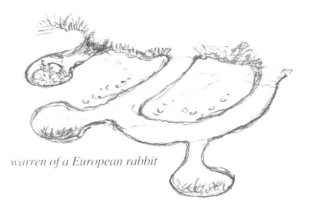

warren of a European rabbit